Wisdom, *Where Are You?*

by:

Reverend Brenda R. Berry
B.A., M.Div.
Pastor Emeritus-NYC. PRESBYTERY, 2019

Book Savvy International Inc.
Success is waiting for you...

All inquirers should be addressed to:

Book Savvy International, Inc.
1626 Clear View Drive, Beverly Hills California 90210, United States
Hotline: (213) 855-4299

https://booksavvyinternational.com/

Ordering Information:

Amount Deals. Special rebates are accessible on the amount bought by corporations, associations, and others. For points of interest, contact the distributor at the address above.

Printed in the United States of America.

ISBN-13   Paperback   979-8-89190-091-2

             eBook   979-8-89190-092-9

Library of Congress Control Number: 2023921812

Dedication

I dedicate this book first to the LORD—Jehovah God, in gratitude for His guidance throughout my life. In retrospect, I can now see how the hand of God has been with me through many dire situations and has brought me safely thus far. To all the teachers who saw their profession as a calling, back then in the Island of Jamaica, W.I., and to those I encountered here in the US at Brooklyn College and the New Brunswick Seminary. I thank God for you and your dedicated service. You instilled confidence in me and encouraged me to strive for the best that was available.

My late mother deserves great credit for working diligently to ensure that my siblings and I received the best education available and possible at that time.

To my two sons, Earl and Noel: I recognize that my call to ministry and all the transitions that it entailed created many challenges in our lives. I appreciate your patience and support when and where you could.

Finally, to my first granddaughter Kendall, and my twin grandchildren Everett and Essence, I give God thanks for you and trust that this book will still be in use as you grow up and that it will become a blessing in your lives.

Acknowledgements

I express much appreciation to two women who spiritually and morally supported me on my ministerial journey during my seminary years and through to my ordination: Rev. Clara Woodson and Rev. Judith Gorsuch. They helped to sustain me with prayers and encouragement. Rev. Woodson was like a spiritual mother to me. Rev. Gorsuch was my "Field Supervisor" as well.

Also, I recognize the members of my weekly small study group where we sharpen one another with Scripture reading, reflections, and prayers throughout the COVID-19 Pandemic season: Kwabena, his wife Stella, Cora, and Adizatu.

PREVIEW

JOB'S DISCOURSE ON WISDOM
(Job 28 paraphrased and abbreviated)

Human beings find ways in, upon, and under the earth to mine silver, refine gold, smelt copper, unearth iron, search the dark recesses of earth for ore. Considering the safety of people, they break open shafts and hang them swinging far away.

In the molten core of the earth, it is turned up like as by fire. Yet from this same earth with a hot molten core, comes bread and all manner of foods for human consumption.

It is the source of precious stones: Sapphires and gold dust, proud lions and other animals pass over it. Men cut out channels of rocks and their eyes see precious things. They damn up streams and bring forth light.

All this human beings do. BUT HERE IS THE QUESTION: "Where can wisdom be found; and where is the place of understanding?

People do not know its value, nor is it known in the land of the living. The deep says: "It is not in me; the sea says: "It is not in me."

It cannot be purchased by silver, gold, or precious stones. From where then does wisdom come, and where is the place of understanding? Destruction and Death say: "We have heard a report about it with our ears." God (alone) understands its ways and knows its place. For He looks to the ends of the earth and sees under the whole heavens. ...Then He saw WISDOM and declared it. ...He prepared it and searched it out.

And to humanity He said:

"Behold, the fear of the LORD —that is wisdom. And to depart from evil is understanding."

Introduction

The Book of Proverbs is the only book of the Bible which is as relevant today as it was when it was first written over 2,000 years ago. It is the only book that tells us clearly and explicitly what it was designed and designated to accomplish in the human heart, life, and mind. Ultimately, it teaches about the kind of character, discipline, and practices that lead to a balanced life of success, well-being, long life, and favor with God and people. Some have fallen victim in the workplace and elsewhere because they have tried to achieve success by "any means necessary." But in Proverbs 3:1-4, King Solomon wrote: "My son, do not forget my teaching, but let your mind retain my commandments; for they will bestow on you—length of days, years of life, and well-being. Let fidelity and steadfastness not leave you. Bind them about your throat. Write them upon the tablet of your mind, and you will find favor and approbation in the eyes of God and man."

This book is primarily written by Solomon, the son of David, with small portions written by Agur and the mother of King Lemuel. Throughout the book, themes like wisdom, knowledge, understanding, obedience, diligence, social etiquette, and moral character, humility, prudence, discernment, honesty, and integrity are repeated many times over to ensure that these qualities are ingrained in the mind from an early age. Proverbs 1:4 clearly tells us that this book is intended to give prudence to the simple, knowledge and discretion to the young men, teach reverence for the Creator God, respect and obedience for parents; because these will lead to successful, upright, and righteous living.

Proper knowledge and understanding of God's Holy Word (but especially of Proverbs) will also teach us how to avoid business failures and deception, teach justice and equity, and how to manage and discern a multitude of other life issues and pitfalls. "Prudence" is one of the themes raised, and according to the *American Heritage Dictionary*, this means to have or to develop the ability to cautiously handle practical matters with the capacity to have advance understanding of probable results or outcome. I would call this having *"foresight."*

Ultimately, according to 1 Corinthians 1:24, *"Jesus is the wisdom and power of God."* He is the Word Incarnate—i.e., the Word that pre-existed time and was with the Father at creation. "He" became flesh and dwelt among us (John 1:1-5, Hebrews 1:1-5). Therefore, the more we know Jesus and know about Him as the Rock of our foundation and of our salvation, the more wisdom, knowledge, understanding, empowerment, and ability we will have to wisely navigate our earthly life's journey. Therefore, it seems right to make the knowledge of God through faith in Christ Jesus, a major *life-time goal.* Psalm 111:10 declares that *"The fear of the LORD is the beginning of wisdom."* As a retired pastor and a mother of two adult sons, I am quite convinced that *the lack of the teaching and knowledge of the Word of God on a consistent basis* in the public square, in the homes, and in our schools has left a vacancy for bad behavior, foolishness, and unrestrained violence in communities, in the government, and in law-enforcement. This book is a *"thirty-one day"* attempt to begin a journey to the seeking and the finding of wisdom one day at a time. The reading of each day's chapter is accompanied by a prayer intended to help the readers to pray for and to get wisdom; and with all their getting to get understanding. May this be a life changing experience according to the divine will and power of Jehovah God in Trinity through Christ Jesus!

It is suggested that the reader concentrate on only one chapter per day with the associated prayer focus on the particular character traits that require transformation—not only for self and family, but for the broader society and world. Prayers may be personalized.

Thirty-One Chapters With Prayers
For Thirty-One Days,
In Pursuit Of Wisdom, Knowledge,
And Understanding

Contents

Proverbs Chapter 1

Day #1

Wisdom begins with the fear or reverence of Jehovah God; for all wisdom originates with and is rooted and grounded in the Creator of the universe. Hebrews 1:2b-3 explains that it is Christ who with the Father made and sustains all things by the power of the Word. It is the Creator who provides for all creatures great and small. It is Christ, the only begotten Son of God, the Father, who purges our sins by His own Blood. Christ is the brightness of the Father's glory and the exact image of His Father's person. Jesus explained further in John 10:30 that He and the Father are one. Therefore, those who would be wise will begin by seeking to know the Creator God through faith in Christ; for, according to Jesus himself—No one comes to the Father except through him.

Psalm 14:1 tells us that it is a fool who says in his heart that there is no God.

1. To receive, to retain, and to apply true wisdom, one must believe that the Creator of the universe self-exists and designs all that exists to honor, glorify, worship, adore, and praise its Creator.

2. When humanity—the highest order of God's creation (made in God's likeness and image)— is separated from Him then the anchor, our foundations crumble, and ultimately, we can be destroyed. People and all creation will go adrift if not connected and anchored to the Creator in Whom

1

all wisdom dwells and from Whom all blessings flow. Let us consider the "insanity" we have been seeing, hearing, and experiencing in recent years and months, and examine from where our society has fallen. Humanity is more than mere flesh and bones.

3. It's a fool and scoffer who despises wisdom, hates knowledge, rejects the guidance of parents, and ignores God's Words (Psalm 53:1). So, I ask: "Wisdom...where are you?"

4. Let knowledge, wisdom, and instruction be as precious ornaments or trinkets worn about the neck. Don't just drift through life like a ship without a compass. Be sure to connect with God through Scripture and by the Holy Spirit in prayer and by faith daily and throughout life. Make plans and prepare well but depend on God to help you to execute them successfully.

5. A warning to the young: Do not associate with sinners and bad companions or gangs who hang about the streets in secret, plotting to do wrong. Do not join in their bloody schemes to entice you to do wicked deeds, for they will endanger you and damage their own lives.

6. Wisdom is in the public square, at the chief concourse, and at the open gates—calling loudly, persistently, and constantly to the simple ones, but they keep ignoring her [wisdom].

7. On those who turn and listen to the voice of wisdom, God will pour out His Spirit and make His Word known to them (Proverbs 1:23).

8. Those who reject the outstretched hand of God's wisdom, ignore His call, and disdain His counsel, His rebuke, and would have none of His wisdom—

on them, terrors will come, as well as storms and destruction as a whirlwind. Distress shall come upon them, for God will not answer them when they call even if they try to seek Him diligently. They will reap the fruit of their disobedience, their own fancies, and complacencies.

9. Whoever listens to wisdom will dwell safely and securely without fear of evil.

PRAYER: *Jehovah God of all wisdom, knowledge, and understanding, we open our hearts and minds to receive Your teaching. In Your mercy, make us receptive to Your instructions so that we do not stumble or fall. In the name of Christ Jesus, please grant us what we need to become wise and not to be foolish. By faith, we believe we have what we ask, for it is in the name of Christ that we lift our prayers to the Throne of Grace and to the Mercy Seat. Hallelujah…Amen!*

Proverbs Chapter 2

Day #2

The value, essence, worth, and effectiveness of wisdom:

1. Godly wisdom is a treasure, for it inspires integrity, humility, courage, and self-discipline, gives direction, promotes understanding, shields and guards the upright, guards the just, and preserves the way of the saints of God.

2. When wisdom enters the heart, then knowledge becomes pleasant to the soul to give understanding, to deliver from evil, immorality, seduction, undue troubles, trials, and untimely death.

3. Keep to the paths of righteousness and so inherit the land and retain it. Therefore, those who practice and pursue upright living will inherit material blessings as well.

4. The wicked and the unfaithful will be cut off and uprooted from the earth.

You may ask: "How does one begin to get this wisdom?" Consider the following:

a. In Proverbs Chapter 1:7-8, King Solomon wrote that wisdom begins with the fear and reverence for God and obedience to the instructions of parents.

b. Proverbs 9:10: "The fear of the Lord is the beginning of wisdom, and knowledge of the Holy One is understanding." Therefore, actively seek to know the Creator God and to learn the ways and teachings of Christ Jesus the Son.

c. Job 28:28: "Behold the fear of the Lord is wisdom; and to depart from evil is understanding."

d. James 1:5: "If any of you lacks wisdom, let him ask of God who will give to all liberally without reproach, and it will be given to her."

e. 1 Kings 3:9: King Solomon said to the Lord: "Therefore, give to Your servant an understanding heart to judge Your people, that I may discern good from evil…" Then the Lord said to him: "Because you have not asked long life, riches, nor asked the life of your enemies, but asked for understanding and wisdom to discern justice, behold I have given you a wise and understanding heart…and I have also given you what you have not asked: both riches and honor…" (1 Kings 3:10-13).

f. Prov. 2:10-11: When wisdom enters the heart, knowledge will be pleasant to the soul. Discretion will preserve you; and understanding will keep you.

PRAYER: *Eternal God, who self-exists and who by wisdom out of nothing created all things seen and unseen, we submit our limited minds and hearts to your infinite intelligence, creativity, divinity, and unsearchable wisdom. Come into our hearts, Lord Jesus, and grant us, we pray, all that is necessary to make us wise, intelligent, discerning, prudent, and humble. Help us, Holy Spirit, to use the talents and gifts given to us for Your glory, honor, and praise; for our own good, and for the good of others, we beseech You in the mighty name of Christ Jesus, who is the wisdom and power of God, and who is the Word incarnate. For these blessings, we give thanks by faith that we have what we ask. Hallelujah…Amen!*

Proverbs Chapter 3

Day #3

Guidance for the young:

Review questions for discussion

- What is the difference between wisdom and knowledge?

- When should parents begin to teach godly wisdom to the young?

I would suggest this: As soon as they can watch TV and begin to react to it, and as soon as they can hear and respond to the voice of their parents. Begin to say blessings over their meals so they know it comes from God through their parents and other loved ones. Begin to show God's love and say, e.g. – *"God is love. God loves me. I belong to God, who created me. I love God, who loves me. All good things come from God, the Creator and Provider of all good things. ... I am a child of God,"* etc. (Of course, use language that is age appropriate.)

According to Proverbs 3:1-2, let the children learn, observe, and retain the knowledge of God's Word in their heart, for it will add long life and peace to them. In Mark 10:14b, we hear Jesus inviting the little children to come to Him and telling His disciples not to forbid them.

Parents and other adults are responsible for teaching them to help them become firmly rooted in mercy and in truth. Bind them on their hearts and wear them like precious jewels about the neck. Thus, you and they will find favor with God and with people (Deuteronomy 6:6-9).

1. Firmly trust and acknowledge God in all circumstances and situations so He can direct our thoughts and paths.

2. No one should assume on his own that they know everything nor make important decisions and plans without seeking help from God and from wise counselors. Do not be wise in your own eyes, but turn to the Lord for help in everything—small or great. ***When in doubt, ask what the Bible has to say about the subject or seek reliable counsel.

3. Fear God. Depart from evil, so you will live healthy lives physically, morally, spiritually, and otherwise.

4. Honor God by returning the first fruits of all our possessions and increase (the tithe and offerings). Then we will abound in abundance, our wine-vats will be full, and our barns will overflow with grain and oil.

5. Learn to humbly accept and obey the correction and counsel of the Lord, for the Lord corrects those He loves.

6. Those who find wisdom and gain understanding find wealth, riches, honor, happiness peace, joy, and life itself with security and confidence.

7. Be generous and kind to the poor when necessary and possible and avoid unnecessary conflict with others, for God's secret counsel is with the righteous.

8. Do not envy the wicked for his house is cursed, but the blessing of the Lord is in the house of the righteous.

9. God scorns the scorner but gives grace to the humble. Make a point of teaching and practicing humility with wisdom, patience, kindness, gentleness, and self-control.

10. The wise shall inherit glory, but the fool—the legacy of shame.

A little friendly advice to parents and other family members: Parents and other family members are encouraged to begin speaking, reading, playing biblical words of life, truth, and wisdom into the hearing, hearts, and minds of their children; for the worldly influences, attractions, and pollutants are too available in our time and society to possess the minds of the young and the vulnerable. Just as we eat natural food to nourish and strengthen our bodies from childhood into adulthood and old age, so we need to feed the spiritual food of the Word of God to children in word, song, play, music, etc. for their spiritual maturity and balance. Let the children see their parents kneel and pray together over them regularly. Psalm 1:1-3 is a good one for them to hear frequently. Ephesians 6:1-3 (for the children) and verse 4 (for the parents). Speak Psalm 23. Say the Lord's Prayer and sing the Doxology regularly in their hearing. Just as they can learn and react to the cartoons so early, so too they can begin to take in the spiritual food for their mind, soul, and spirit. It can become health for their minds, bones, and flesh over time and for eternity.

PRAYER: *O Lord, Jehovah God, in Your steadfast love and mercy please release Your truth into the hearts and minds of Your little ones and to all of us. Make us receptive to Your Spirit and to Your words of wisdom, we pray. Let us be guided and directed by Your Holy Spirit all the days of our lives, we ask. May You grant more than we could ever desire, ask, think, or imagine, for we lift our prayers to You by faith and with thanksgiving through Christ Jesus! Hallelujah…Amen!*

Proverbs Chapter 4

Day #4

A question for reflection and discussion:

- What do you think of this comment (excuse) some parents make: "Oh, leave them [the children] alone. When they get older, they will choose for themselves!"

The goal is to encourage youngsters to heed their parents' instructions through the knowledge of the Word of God. It is also fitting for adults to retain wisdom for life and for health. The key words here: Godly parental discipline and correction, discernment, teachings of the Commandments of God, and the practice of obedience to them.

1. Listen and retain, obey, and apply the teachings of parents, wise counselors, and teachers, for by them you shall live life successfully.

2. Seek and acquire wisdom and discernment. Cling to them and hug them to yourself and be consistent, for they will bring you honor and adorn you with grace and a glorious crown.

3. Hold fast to discipline and wisdom and do not let go, for it is your life.

4. Stay away from evil people. Turn away from them who make it their goal to hurt others by their wickedness and lawlessness.

5. The path of the righteous is brightly lit like sunshine at noon. Try to stay on this path.

6. Those who seek, find, and cling to wisdom, discernment, obedience to parental instructions (if godly), and avoid evil deeds with evil influences, will guard your minds and find the source of life.

7. Keep unclean and devious speech out of your mouth.

8. Keep your eyes straight ahead. Focus on your way and survey your path so you will prosper.

9. Keep your feet from evil. In other words—do not go where evil is. Run the other way!

10. Wisdom is the principal thing. Therefore, seek it with all your heart as if life depended on it. Get wisdom, cling to her, and so gain understanding.

11. Wisdom will crown you with grace and glory and deliver you in time of need.

12. Keep wisdom in your heart for in it is life and health.

COMMENT: Let the knowledge of the Word of God penetrate and permeate the heart and mind to produce discernment, prudence, wise counsel, discretion, patience, strength, kindness, gentleness, and self- control. When wisdom enters the heart, knowledge becomes pleasant to the soul. When we stumble or stray, the Word of God in our hearts will cause us to reflect and to return to the source of life and wisdom. Remember 1 Corinthians 1:24b-25, "Christ the power of God and the wisdom of God…" So, endeavor to keep Him in our thoughts and hearts.

PRAYER: *Jehovah God in trinity—You are pure light. In the name of Christ Jesus, we ask that You shine the light of Your countenance upon us and enlighten our minds that we will hunger and thirst after righteousness and be filled. In Your loving kindness and tender mercies, begin to bless the youngest to the oldest of us with Your truth,*

Your knowledge, and with Your understanding, that we will be made wise and strong in faith. Grant us grace, we pray, to apply and to use what You give to us for Your glory, honor, and praise; for our good, and for the good of others. We receive what we ask, for we ask all things in the mighty name of Christ Jesus with faith and with gratitude. Hallelujah...Amen!

Proverbs Chapter 5

Day #5

Further instructions and guidance for the young:

It is specifically directed to virile young men and all younger people seeking relationships to warn them against immoral, fleshly living and the consequences and life-time regrets that may be the result of bad choices and decisions:

1. To warn them of the danger of adultery

2. To teach them how to identify the immoral and seductive woman

3. To show them the folly of disobedience if they do not follow instruction. They may live to regret it in the end.

KEY: Therefore, be exhorted to study wisdom, gain understanding, discretion, and knowledge. Retain honor, dignity, and mutual respect. Try to build regular Bible study into your schedule. Maintain good Christian fellowship, prayer, and spiritual support in your daily lives, activities, and plans (see Joshua 1:8-9).

The signs of the immoral woman:

1. Her lips drip with words as sweet as honey and her mouth is as smooth as oil.

2. In the end, she is as bitter as wormwood and gall.

3. Her feet lead down to death and her steps to hell.

4. Her ways are unstable, deceptive, and difficult to discover.

5. Do not go near her house door, lest you be ensnared and find that foreigners take your wealth, your body consumes away, and you mourn with regret. (This should scare a few people!)

6. So, let your heart and mind be inclined to be obedient and receptive to the teachings of parents, wise counselors, and teachers. For those who fail to do so, come to total destruction, shame, and ruination publicly.

7. Have your own wife, be satisfied with her love and affection, enjoy her, and let your family be blessed. Do not give your love, wealth, health, affection, and loyalty to the seductress or other immoral people.

8. Be assured that God observes the ways of human-beings and ponders their paths. Jehovah knows that people are entrapped by their own iniquities and are caught in their own sins. They die prematurely, due to lack of obedience, wisdom, knowledge, and understanding. In folly, they are led astray into destruction.

People often become entrapped because they do not know how to avoid snares of deception. because of a lack of knowledge, a lack of spiritual and emotional control over the flesh, disobedience to the wise instructions of parents and teachers, the lust of the flesh and the pride of life. Therefore, seek wisdom and cling fast to her [wisdom], for she is your life.

According to the doctrine of the New Testament in John 3:16-17, *"God so loved the world that he gave his only begotten son so that whoever believes on him would not perish but have everlasting life...for God sent not his Son into the world to condemn the world, but that the world through Him might be saved."* Jesus taught that sin originates in the heart before it is ever enacted. So even the thought of adultery defiles the person. Therefore, our only hope is God's mercy through faith in Christ and the help of the Holy Spirit. Matthew 11:11 tells us that the least in the kingdom of heaven is greater than John the Baptist, because of what Christ did for us. Mark 16:16 tells us that whoever believes and is baptized will be saved. He who does not believe will be condemned.

So, here is the point: While we should do our best to obey the Commandments of God, it is likely, even certain, that we will fall short from time to time. Grace and mercy are guaranteed only by faith in Christ. He has completed the work of our redemption. Those who believe in Him and are saved will not be condemned. This is the big reason we praise and thank Him, appreciate Him, honor, and adore Him so much for our salvation, because He did perfectly what we could not do perfectly. When the Pharisees brought the woman caught in adultery for Jesus to judge and condemn her, He told them to let those who were without sin cast the first stone. They all slithered away without a word. Jesus asked her, *"Did no one condemn you?"* She answered, *"No master."* He said to her, *"Neither do I. Go and sin no more."* Jesus did not condone the sin, but He forgave it. Romans 8:1-2 reminds us that now there is no condemnation to those who are in Christ Jesus.

PRAYER: *Jehovah God in trinity, may You help us not to condemn ourselves or others, but to cast all our cares, worries, concerns, shame, and guilt on Christ Jesus who has completed the work of our redemption on the cross. Thank You, Abba/Father, for Jesus the Christ, Your Son. We thank Him, love Him, and appreciate Him, who first loved us and gave Himself to die for us. O for grace to love Him more! Hallelujah...Amen!*

Proverbs Chapter 6

Day #6

Wise counsel for business matters and co-signing of a debt:

We are warned to protect ourselves from deception and loss that might cause financial ruin and bring one to poverty. Avoid idleness but with diligence and wisdom prepare for the future. Beware of the trap of sexual immorality. Seven things that God hates. The blessings of obedience. Although some of these themes are repeated throughout the book, consider the fact that repetition is a learning tool similar to meditation that helps to solidify information and help the memory to retain facts. For the heart and the mind to change, it often requires repetition. Sometimes we think we have it, but it has not really registered.

1. Do not make verbal, written, or hand-shake pledges to become surety for another's debt; for this could be very dangerous to you and to the well-being of your family. If this has already been done, do all within your power to untangle yourself from such a trap.

2. Observe the instinctive diligence and prudence of a tiny ant and be guided in your own way by it. It has no leader, ruler, or supervisor; yet it gathers supplies in summer and builds up harvest for the winter. Look toward the future and prepare for the days ahead.

3. Do not be a sluggard, you sleepy head! Rise from your laziness and slumber, lest poverty comes upon you like an armed camp.

4. Ways to know the character of the wicked and see that you do not emulate them: The worthless/ wicked person has a perverse mouth, winks the eye, shuffles the feet, points with the finger, is devious in the heart, devises evil continually, sows discord among brothers and sisters.

5. The recompense of the wicked: Their calamity shall come upon them suddenly, and they shall be broken without remedy.

6. The seven things God hates are: 1.) A proud look. 2.) A lying tongue. 3.) Hands that shed innocent blood. 4.) A devious and wicked heart that plans evil. 5.) Feet swift to run to evil. 6.) A false witness that tells lies. 7.) The one who sows discord among the brethren.

7. Beware of adultery: Again...listen, observe, take heed to the godly instructions of godly and wise parents, teachers, and counselors. Cling to them and wear them like precious jewels and fine clothing. Gird them on the heart, waking and sleeping. All sin is offensive to God, but the sin of adultery is particularly dangerous and destructive to families.

8. Learn and digest the Word of God, so it shall become like a lamp unto the feet and a light unto our paths to guide our lives: 1.) It will help to keep young men from seductive women which can become like taking fire into one's bosom. 2.) The writer asks: "Can a person take fire into one's bosom and not be burned, or walk on hot coals and his feet not be seared?"

9. Consequences for disobedience to the Law of God: Even if one steals for a rational reason, if caught, there will be consequences, so it is if one commits adultery. He takes fire to his own bosom, for he destroys his own soul and his family life. The wrath and vengeance of the husband or wife in the case of adultery is justified. Avoid it like a plague!

PRAYER: *In the name of Christ Jesus, who is the wisdom and power of God, we beseech You Jehovah God of all flesh, to infuse us all, but especially the young men, with a spirit of discernment to see, to know, and to take heed according to Your Word, so that we will not be ensnared and entrapped by deception and an immoral lifestyle that can destroy entire lives and entire families. Also, we ask that You break from everyone who has the sluggish spirit of sleep and a lack of vision for a hopeful future that might cause poverty to come upon them as an armed camp. We give thanks to You in the name of Christ Jesus, Jehovah God in trinity. Hallelujah...Amen!*

Proverbs Chapter 7

Day #7

Further exhortation against immorality, seduction, deception, flattery, and adultery.

1. King Solomon instructs and warns his son against the immoral woman and entreats him to call wisdom a sister and understanding a near relative.

2. Learn and obey God's Word, Law, Commands, Precepts as the apple of the eye, and you will be kept safe from crafty and deceptive people.

3. Young men devoid of wisdom and understanding are easily ensnared and trapped by seductive women. The same is true for young women who do not have the Word of God within.

4. The manner and demeanor of a seductress: She is loud, vulgar, and rebellious.

5. She is constantly in the streets, hardly ever at home. She has an impudent face and speaks seemingly sincere words to him to entice him to her bed although she may be married and her husband is away.

6. The consequence and result of yielding to her temptations: He went after her like an ox to the slaughter, or a fool to the correction of the stocks. He did not know it would cost him his life as if

struck with an arrow in the liver or snared like a bird in a trap.

7. Listen to wise counsel, young men: Do not go after such women for they have slain many strong men. ...Their house leads to hell and to the chambers of death.

QUESTIONS:

• How serious are these instructions, and how necessary are they for living a clean and successful life?

• Who is imparting this kind of information, warning, and instruction to the youth of today?

• When should these principles begin to be taught and by whom?

• In what way might a man be responsible for what happens to him because of his choices and free will?

COMMENT: *"Train up a child in the way he should go and when he is old he will not depart from it"* (Proverbs 22:6). Start implanting the Word of God and begin to teach godly principles as early as possible into the hearts and minds of children so that it grows up in them and with them. It will help to form and to frame their characters, and to build their minds and spirits in making life's choices.

PRAYER: *Come, Holy Spirit, and inspire, instruct, and teach parents and the youth in every generation so that we will be guided by godly principles and be empowered to live blessed lives. We pray this in faith and with thanksgiving unto You, Abba/Father in the name of Christ Jesus. The world is desperately in need of You in these times, for worldly and secular knowledge are not enough to deliver us from all manner of evil. Hear our prayer, O Jehovah our God, and attend unto our cries, we beseech You in the name of Christ Jesus! Hallelujah... Amen!*

Proverbs Chapter 8

Day #8

The excellency, eternal riches, and value of wisdom, personified as a female "she:"

1. She [wisdom], is crying out from the top of the hill, in the marketplace, in the square, and at the gates of the city. She is calling to the simple, the foolish, and to all who lack understanding, prudence, discretion, and discernment.

2. God is calling all people to come to Him and to get to know Him so we will not be like lost sheep without a shepherd.

3. The mouth of the wise speak truth and righteousness, and nothing perverse nor crooked will come out of it.

4. Wisdom is better than choice silver, fine gold, or precious stones. Nothing can compare with her.

5. Included in wisdom is found – prudence, discernment, wise counsel, understanding, knowledge, discretion, strength, riches, honor, and good judgement.

6. God hates arrogance but is near to the humble and loves those who love wisdom. He causes them to inherit wealth and fills their treasuries with good.

7. Wisdom originated with the Creator before the beginning of time, and by wisdom God created all that exist: vegetation, animals, waters, land, fountains, clouds etc. Wisdom was like a master craftsman rejoicing in the inhabited world.

8. Seek wisdom daily, listen for her constantly; for whoever finds wisdom, finds life, and obtains the favor of the Lord Jehovah our God.

9. All who hate wisdom, sin against their own soul and love death.

COMMENT: We can study all the books of the world and gain knowledge but never find wisdom. The only source of wisdom is to know Jehovah God through faith in Christ Jesus, the Way, the Truth, and the Life; the Door, the Light, and our Salvation. To those who believe in Him, He will reveal the Father and lead them into the heavenly kingdom where the goodness, favor, love, mercy, peace, rest, and light of God exist. The Bible is the only book that teaches godly wisdom. There are many books about the Bible (commentaries, etc.). However, one must read and learn the Bible itself prayerfully. It needs to be a life-long endeavor... a manual for life, a source book of truth and guidance. Those who ask, seek, and knock will receive. Unfortunately, today, it is no longer taught in schools, and prayer is not allowed.

PRAYER: *Lord, Jehovah God in trinity, grant us, our children, our religious, and government leaders the wisdom that empowers us to live life in health, with prosperity and success, through faith in Your Son, Christ Jesus. Let our hearts and minds be open and receptive to Your voice and to Your Word, we ask. We receive it now and give You thanks for your generosity and kindness. Hallelujah...Amen!*

Proverbs Chapter 9

Day #9

Maturing in wisdom:

When wisdom is built up in a person, he will begin to be like a well-grounded house with strong pillars. When wisdom is practiced, then life is more likely to be successful. It will be like a house fully furnished with all manner of good things, and as a table well spread with the best of food, wine, and drink. Wisdom cries out to the simple and foolish, urging them to keep asking always for more. She calls them to come and eat of her bread, drink of her wine, to forsake foolishness and to live in the way of understanding.

1. The wise person will learn from correction and heed instruction.

2. Teach a just person, and he will increase in understanding.

3. To fear or reverence Lord Jehovah God is the beginning of wisdom and is to be a lifelong endeavor.

4. Those who find wisdom increase their years and quality of life.

5. Foolish men get ensnared and trapped in immorality by clamorous, deceptive, seductive women who hang out in the streets seeing who they can capture. They entreat the foolish to come into their bed which is a web of sin.

COMMENT: To develop and grow in wisdom, we must gain understanding by knowing God through fearing and reverencing Him.

- Study and learn God's ways according to Scripture.

- Ask for the help of Holy Spirit to guide us in the study of the Word and to give us clarity and understanding as we pray and study daily.

- Not everything in the Bible is crystal clear. Sometimes we will need to dig and search diligently to find relevance and meaning. Sometimes we will need to seek the help of godly teachers, counselors, and books.

- Those who seek God the Father will find wisdom through faith in God the Son and by the help of the Holy Spirit.

PRAYER: *Come, Holy Spirit, and guide us into all truth, we pray! Teach us and show us the way to life-abundant and life-eternal. Open our eyes, ears, and hearts to the knowledge and wisdom of God, and cause our minds and our spirits to retain what we learn. Help us to practice it faithfully and consistently. In the name of the One who is the embodiment of the wisdom and power of the Almighty Jehovah God, Christ Jesus our Lord and Savior, we pray. Hallelujah...Amen!*

Proverbs Chapter 10

Day #10

Wise sayings:

The wise versus the foolish person and the rewards of the wise versus the consequence of foolish behavior and actions. "Righteousness" is that which is morally right, just, authentic, and true; is of integrity of character, trustworthy, dependable, and reliable.

1. The wise versus the foolish child and their effect on their parents: gladness or sadness.

2. Treasures built up by wickedness come to nothing, but righteousness delivers from death. God will take care of the righteous and will never let them be famished. The opposite is true for the wicked.

3. The result of a slack hand versus that of the diligent: the slack hand comes to poverty but the diligent brings riches and prosperity.

4. The legacy and the memory of the righteous is blessed with a good name, but the memory of the wicked will be rottenness.

5. There is security and integrity in obeying the commands of God, but fools who stray will fall. Those who are perverted cause trouble and wink the eye, but they will be exposed.

6. Love covers shame but hate stirs up strife.

7. The mouth of the righteous speaks wisdom, but destruction comes from foolish lips and is devoid of understanding.

8. The wise restrains his lips, but fools have a multitude of words and die for lack of wisdom.

9. The blessing of the Lord makes rich, and no sorrow is added to it.

10. Accept instruction and correction and you will live.

11. Whoever hates or slanders is a fool and fools die for lack of wisdom.

12. To a fool, doing evil is like a sport, but the person of understanding has wisdom and hates evil.

13. What the wicked fears most will come upon them, and their days will be shortened, but the desire of the righteous will be granted with gladness.

14. The wicked will not inherit the earth.

15. A lazy servant is toxic to his employer like vinegar to the teeth.

16. The wise who fear the Lord prolong their days, experience gladness, and gain strength.

PRAYER: *Jehovah God in trinity, by Your wisdom You created all things, including humanity. You created us in Your own likeness and image. However, because sin has separated us from You, we do not function as wisely as we ought. We pray that, by Your Holy Spirit, You might grant us Your grace of wisdom, knowledge, and understanding. Help us, especially the young, to seek You first, know Christ, and study Him, so that we will obey Your Commandments, Your Word, and Your holy will. Then we will be enabled to live strong and blessed lives that honor You, others, and ourselves. In the name of Christ Jesus, we lift our requests and petitions with thanksgiving and by faith. Hallelujah...Amen!*

Proverbs Chapter 11

Day #11

Integrity, honesty, result of having a generous spirit, riches, and wealth.

1. Honesty in business (a just scale) is a delight to God versus dishonesty which is an abomination to the Lord.

2. Pride always precedes a fall, but humility brings wisdom.

3. Integrity builds up and guides the upright, but perversity and disloyalty destroy.

4. The hopes and expectations of the wicked perish when they die, but the righteous are delivered from trouble.

5. When the righteous prospers, the city rejoices, and when the wicked perish, there is jubilation.

6. Apply wisdom and understanding in controlling the tongue so that peace might prevail and strife ceases.

7. In the multitude of counsel, there is security and safety. Again, do not secure a debt note for a stranger, for it could lead to financial ruination.

8. A gracious woman is honored. A seemingly lovely woman who lacks discretion is like putting a ring in a pig's snout.

9. The generous person will be made rich, and whoever waters will be watered. There is a good reward for the righteous and generous person which leads to life.

10. There are those who scatter—and it leads to abundance, and there are those who hoard everything and have nothing.

11. Those who trust in riches will fall, but the righteous who trust in God will flourish.

COMMENT: These themes are repeated throughout the book of Proverbs, comparing the fate of the stingy, the wicked, the disloyal, unfaithful, and the greedy with the blessings and rewards of the righteous here on earth. This may be to ensure that the lessons become familiar and are instilled in our mind and in our heart that we may be empowered to avoid pitfalls on our life's journey.

PRAYER: *God of all wisdom, knowledge, and understanding, in Your generosity and kindness, we ask that You release to us the ability to make good choices that lead to godliness, success, and prosperity. Help us to identify, renounce, and reject all that is false and destructive. In Your mercy, may You hear and answer us speedily, we pray in faith and with thanksgiving through Christ Jesus, the author and finisher of our faith. Hallelujah…Amen!*

Proverbs Chapter 12

Day #12

God's favor toward the righteous and His disfavor against the wicked:

The good and righteous person – accepts instruction, loves knowledge, has favor with God, is stable and rooted, and bears good fruit. Their spouse is a crown to their head, their mouth delivers them through wisdom. The righteous tend their flock and cultivate their field. They are satisfied and are delivered from trouble.

1. The prudent person covers shame and conceals knowledge, is diligent, and rules over the lazy, who will be put to shame.

2. Anxiety causes depression, but a good word makes the heart glad.

3. The righteous choose their friends carefully.

4. Diligence is a precious possession of the righteous that leads to life.

5. The righteous are established, rooted, and cannot be moved. It is not so for the wicked.

6. An excellent wife does her husband good, but the spouse who causes shame is like rottenness to his bones.

7. The righteous are humble, compassionate, truthful, and diligent. Their houses will stand in times of trouble. They will be productive and prosper. They care even for their animals. But the wicked who are cruel, who lie, who are lazy, and deceitful will not prosper for long.

PRAYER: *Jehovah God in Christ Jesus, we thank You for Your love, guidance, protection, and wisdom. In Your mercy, may You heal our hearts and minds and make us receptive to Your Word of truth. Please open our understanding so that we might gain knowledge and retain wisdom. Make us like the righteous and take away foolishness from us, we pray. For these blessings, we ask in the strong and mighty name of Your Son, Christ Jesus, with thanksgiving and by faith we consider it done. Hallelujah...Amen!*

Proverbs Chapter 13

Day #13

Scripture tells us that a person without self-control is like a city without walls and that the power of life and death are in the tongue. Therefore, heed wise counsel, and listen to parental instruction. It is important to develop and to maintain a godly character of integrity and moral standards that model the principles of a righteous and Holy God.

1. Again—the righteous listen to wise counsel, guard their speech, and are generous with their riches. Therefore, light shines upon their paths.

2. They gain their wealth honestly, realize their hopes and desires, and they practice that which produces life.

3. They gain favor with God and with people, for they act with wisdom, knowledge, and understanding.

4. Poverty and shame will not come to the righteous because they heed wise counsel.

5. Those who walk with the wise will become wise, but fools stumble and are destroyed.

6. The righteous leave an inheritance for their grandchildren, but the wealth of the foolish is stored up for the inheritance of the righteous.

7. Injustice causes the abundance of food produced by the poor to be wasted.

8. Wise parents who love their children will discipline them promptly, but those who hate their children will spoil them.

9. The righteous are always satisfied, but the wicked will always be in want.

10. There are those who hoard everything in order to be rich, yet they have nothing; there are those who give and scatter but have much.

11. The display of pride leads to strife. Instead, let wisdom and good advice be our guide.

12. Hold on to hope even when it is delayed. Keep hope alive until the desire is fulfilled. It will bring joy like a tree of life.

13. Aim to be a wise and faithful ambassador instead of a wicked messenger.

14. Those who adhere to the Commandments of God will find the fountain of life and will be rewarded with goodness.

15. The righteous and diligent will have enough to satisfy their souls, but the wicked and lazy will suffer hunger and poverty.

PRAYER: *Omniscient God of all knowledge, wisdom, and understanding, grant us wisdom for these days, we pray. Help the diligent and the faithful to see as You see, and to do as You would have them to do. Let Your Word be applied and appropriated by Your Holy Spirit into our hearts and minds that we may become light and salt in Your world. Grant us the wisdom that leads to true wealth. Through the matchless name of Christ Jesus, we give thanks by faith for these blessings. Hallelujah... Amen!*

Proverbs Chapter 14

Day #14

God's favor is upon the wise, versus God's disfavor toward the foolish, continued:

1. The wise build up their house (and by extension, life, and family) and do not tear it down. But the foolish, prideful, and perverse tear it down with their own hands.

2. Much increase comes through the strength, discipline, and diligence of the worker. Their trough will be full, but the trough is clean [empty] where these are lacking.

3. The false witness and the liar will not find wisdom and understanding, for God despises lying.

4. The foolish mock at sin and are deceitful. They will not flourish. When you find out who they are, avoid them.

5. The foolish and the backslider act on their own advice that seems right to them, but it leads to wrong and fruitless paths.

6. The self-confident, quick-tempered person acts foolishly. They inherit the fruit of folly, while the prudent are crowned with knowledge. The wise are slow to wrath, but the foolish are impulsive and hasty.

7. Whoever oppresses the poor is a reproach to their Creator.

8. The children of those who fear the Lord will have confidence and find a place of refuge. They will find a fountain of life.

9. A king who has a multitude of people is honored, but a lack of people is the downfall of a prince. Yet our trust cannot be in people but must be in God first and foremost.

10. One who is slow to wrath gets understanding, but the impulsive are foolish.

11. Righteousness exalts a nation, but sin is a reproach to any people.

12. Do not harbor envy in the heart, for it is like rottenness to the bones and the Lord will not hear our prayers. David prayed: *"Create in me a clean heart ...O God and renew a right and steadfast spirit within me"* (Psalm 51: 10). We too can pray this same prayer for ourselves as well.

PRAYER: *Omniscient, omnipotent, and omnipresent God, in Your steadfast love and mercy, turn our hearts and minds toward that which is wise and fruitful and away from what is destructive and foolish, we pray in the name of Christ Jesus, who is the wisdom and power of God. It is Christ who won victory over the flesh and the carnal mind for us. We can run to Him, and we are saved when we feel overwhelmed. Where Adam and Eve failed, He overcame. Therefore, we receive what we ask in the name of Christ Jesus, our Messiah. May we receive more than we could ever imagine, ask, or think. Hallelujah...Amen!*

Proverbs Chapter 15

Day #15

The effect of the speech, the tongue, and the lips of the righteous versus that of the foolish and the arrogant:

1. The wise and righteous give a soft answer and so turn away from wrath, but the foolish answers with anger and cause strife.

2. The righteous receive instruction and their tongues are like a tree of life. As a result, there is abundance of treasure and wealth in their houses.

3. The prayers of the righteous are a delight to God, but those of the foolish are an abomination.

4. God judges and observes the hearts and intentions of people. Therefore, come to God in humility and in truth, with confession, repentance, forgiveness, clean hands, and a clean heart.

5. The hearts of the righteous seek knowledge and understanding, but those of the foolish feeds on foolishness.

6. Those of merry heart are like a continual feast. They spread joy and life to many friends.

7. It is better to have a little and have peace than to have a lot with trouble.

8. A wrathful man without self-control is dangerous and stirs up strife, but he who is slow to anger avoids contention.

9. The way of life for the righteous points upward that they might turn away from the evil below.

10. God does not prosper the well-being of the proud, the arrogant, and the greedy, but loves to lavish blessings on the humble.

11. Without godly counsel, plans cannot prosper and be successful.

12. The favor of God is toward the righteous and He hears their prayers; but He does not answer the wicked.

13. Those who are greedy for gain and practice bribery will find trouble in their own homes.

14. God gives honor to the humble but not to the arrogant.

PRAYER: *Jehovah God in Trinity, all good things come from You. In Your steadfast love and mercy, we ask that You transform our minds and hearts to be more like You. Help us to control our tongues and attitudes to conform to Your will and to Your ways. Transform our thoughts and actions that we may be conformed to learn wisdom, gain understanding, and to live with peace, in humility, contentment, well-being, and success. Help us to fear You and to love others as we ought. In the name of Christ Jesus, change us from the inside and cause it to reflect on the outside—we beseech You, so that we might live victoriously and joyfully all our days. With thanksgiving and with faith, we lift this prayer to You, Abba/Father, expecting a true change and transformation in our lives. Hallelujah...Amen!*

Proverbs Chapter 16

Day #16

The result of making plans and decisions without God's counsel, guidance, and instruction:

Form partnership with God in preparing our plans, for the Lord is the one who will give answers and cause them to prosper. Use wisdom in dealing with rulers and kings that you might receive favor and acceptance with God and with man. King Solomon repeats over and over the qualities of the wise and righteous that lead to prosperity in life, such as humility, a wise tongue, a joyful attitude, wisdom, knowledge, understanding, reverence for God, obedience to God's Word, mercy, truth, pleasant words, diligence in labor, patience, self-control, etc. These please God and create an atmosphere for blessings to flow into one's life.

1. The wise seek God's guidance in making their decisions and plans for their future. On our own, we tend to think our own thoughts and ways are right. This is prideful which is offensive to God. We should already know that God avoids the arrogant.

2. When a person's way pleases God, He makes even his enemies to be at peace with him. The Lord directs their steps.

3. Kings should rule and speak carefully with authority and honesty, for their words carry great weight. It is an abomination for kings and rulers to

commit wickedness, for thrones are established by
righteousness.

4. It is better to seek and find wisdom and understanding
   than to have silver and gold.

5. Haughtiness and pride precede embarrassment,
   debasement, and fall.

6. Trust in God, develop a prudent heart, use wise
   words of the lips, and this will help to produce
   happiness. Do not be like the ungodly, who stir
   up evil, sow strife, separate best friends, and are
   deceptive to their neighbors.

7. The grey hair of the elderly is a crown of glory and
   a sign of righteousness. So, it is prudent to show
   respect for them and listen to their counsel.

8. The wise are slow to anger and they practice self-
   control.

9. Ultimately, after all our human efforts, it is God
   who has the final say.

QUESTION: How and why should we seek guidance from
God when we are making significant plans for our lives and
even for our daily activities?

PRAYER: *Jehovah God, Creator of the universe, in wisdom
You made all things. Omnipotent, omnipresent, and omniscient God, if
we could, we would make ourselves wise and effectively change ourselves.
But we find ourselves to be inadequate. Therefore, we ask for the help
of the Holy Spirit in the name of Christ Jesus to change our hearts and
minds so that we will comply with Your will. Mold us and shape us after
Thine own will, we pray. Correct our broken ways and fix our bad habits,
we beseech You. Grant us all the grace that we need to become all that
we ought to be, so that we may become acceptable in Your sight and find
favor in Your presence. In the name of the risen Christ Jesus, we lift these
prayers in faith and with thanksgiving, expecting to experience a true*

transformation of character and attitude in the likeness of Christ Jesus our Lord. Hallelujah...Amen!

Proverbs Chapter 17

Day #17

Advice and admonition about the foolish versus the wise:

We see the life of strife of the evil doers with lying lips and how God views them. On the other hand, we see how God views the honest, the loving, the wise, the merciful, and those who know how to control their speech wisely.

1. A wise servant is more valuable than a foolish son and stands to inherit more among brothers.

2. Those who mock the poor and are glad about calamity will be punished.

3. Whoever covers a transgression seeks love, but whoever repeats a matter separates friends.

4. Do not reward evil for good, for then evil will not depart from your house.

5. A good friend loves and is faithful at all times.

6. Again—do not make a pledge to be responsible for someone else's debt.

7. It is wrong to punish the righteous or to strike a righteous prince.

8. Those with a calm spirit have understanding and are seen as wise.

9. It is better to live in peace and have a little than to live with plenty in a house filled with strife.

10. As silver and gold are refined in a furnace, so God refines the human heart.

11. Jehovah God punishes those who mock the poor, so do not ridicule or disrespect them.

12. Giving and receiving presents is a precious and pleasant thing. It helps to promote prosperity and goodwill.

13. Do all we can to stop quarrelling and strife before they begin.

14. A deceitful heart and a perverse tongue can only produce what is evil.

15. Endeavor to keep a merry heart, for it is like medicine to the soul; but a broken spirit dries the bones.

16. It is best to keep a calm spirit and a quiet tongue of few words. Even a foolish person who keeps his tongue is often perceived to be wise.

PRAYER: *Jehovah God, repetition is one way of helping us to retain the essence and impact of the lessons we need to learn. In Your steadfast love and mercy, please cause Your Holy Spirit to anoint our hearts and minds to make the necessary changes in the ways we live, think, and act; in how we treat others, how we use our mouths for good or for evil. Fill us, we pray, with Your wisdom so that we will reflect godliness to others in the world, that we will make good and wise choices and decisions for our lives and let us be successful in all our plans. We thank You, Abba/Father, for transforming our minds, hearts, souls, and spirits as children of God in the world; for it is in the name of Christ Jesus that we lift our prayers to You in faith and with thanksgiving. Hallelujah... Amen!*

Proverbs Chapter 18

Day #18

The words, thoughts, and actions of a foolish and wicked person versus those of the prudent, the patient, and the humble.

1. The foolish separates and isolates himself from the wise counsel, for he delights in the expressions of his own heart.

2. The foolish bring contempt, reproach, and dishonor with them wherever they go. Their lips breathe contention, and their mouths speak destruction.

3. The slothful worker is likened to a destroyer, and the words of a talebearer are like tasty trifles that go down deeply into the body.

4. The righteous run into the name of the Lord for refuge—because God's name is like a strong tower—not the worship of material wealth and idols.

5. Haughtiness brings destruction, but humility brings honor.

6. The wise listen well before speaking on a matter. They seek and acquire knowledge and keep a cheerful spirit that sustains them.

7. Resolve matters and avoid offenses among brothers and friends, and let your mouth speak fruitful words

that lead to satisfaction. "Blessed are the peace-makers..." (Matthew 5:)

8. Be careful with the use of the tongue because it can speak life or death (Proverbs 18:21). Commit to use the tongue to speak life and whatever is positive, true, and praise-worthy, but not to promote quarrels, contentions, or strife.

9. It is a good and blessed thing for a man to find a wife. It is a sign of favor from the Lord.

10. It is better to use entreaties than to answer roughly.

11. To have friends, one must first become a friend, for there is a friend who sticks closer than a brother.

12. There is power and deliverance for believers in using, applying, and calling upon the name of Christ Jesus with faith and with authority.

13. Our gifts and talents when properly applied will bring us before great, influential, and godly people.

14. Do not be quick to judge until both sides of an argument are heard.

15. Rich or poor, avoid using abusive language that is offensive, but choose entreaties instead.

16. Those who would have friends must be friendly.

PRAYER: *Merciful and gracious God of all creation, we turn to You regularly for the help of your Holy Spirit to mold us and to shape us after Thy will. We desire to experience Your favor, but at times we miss the mark and fall short of Your glory. You invite us to Your banquet table filled with heavenly things. So, we come in the name of Christ Jesus, our Way-Maker, our Good Shepherd, our Mediator, Intercessor, and Great High Priest. We beseech You, Abba/Father, in His name to grant us wisdom, knowledge, discernment, prudence, humility, faith, love, guidance, and direction for every day. Sanctify our tongues and speech so that we will* *say what You want us to say to bring life to others. All these mercies we ask by faith and with thanksgiving through Christ Jesus. Hallelujah... Amen!*

Proverbs Chapter 19

Day #19

There are possible snares and traps in trying to use worldly goods to gain favor and influence with people. Instead practice diligence, honesty, and faithfulness, and respect civil and parental authority.

1. It is better to be poor and have a good character of integrity, than to be rich and be perverse.

2. A person's wealth may attract people to him, but poverty tends to cause isolation.

3. The discerning are slow to anger, and they overlook transgressions.

4. The wise servant avoids the wrath of the king with persuasive words.

5. The inheritance of property is from parents and other ancestors, but a good and wise wife comes from God.

6. Whoever lends to the poor, lends to God and will be duly rewarded.

7. Correct and train children while there is hope.

8. Do not rescue the foolish person who is prone to wrath, for you will just have to do it again.

9. Seek counsel from the Lord and from those who are trained in godly wisdom.

10. Kindness and fear of the Lord leads to life.

11. The lazy person won't even try to help himself to eat his own food.

12. Listen to wise instruction, seek justice, avoid scoffers and people of ill-repute, avoid quarrels. Instead, seek peace and pursue it.

PRAYER: *O Lord, Jehovah God, in Your steadfast love and mercy, grant us your wisdom from above that we might know how to live successfully, peacefully, honestly, and truthfully here on earth. Help us to choose right over wrong and good over evil, we pray. Teach us Your ways, dear God of all wisdom, knowledge, and understanding. We pray by faith in Christ Jesus, who is the Wisdom and Power of God. We give thanks for what You have done and will continue to do. Hallelujah...Amen!*

Proverbs Chapter 20

Day #20

In business matters be sober, honest and trustworthy. Avoid laziness. Keep an examined heart and be true to self, God, and others. It will be like a lamp to the soul.

1. Do not be drunk with wine, it can be deceptive. Yet Psalm 104:1 tells us that wine comes from God to make the heart of man glad or merry. Temperance is to be the goal. The abuse of wine or other strong drink can lead to shame and embarrassment. We are not to allow ourselves to be deceived by it. (See also Proverbs 31:1-6, the advice of King Lemuel's mother about the effect of strong drink and how it might adversely affect good judgement.) It may be best to avoid it all together.

2. Wisdom is associated with the grey hair of the elderly, but physical strength is related to the young.

3. It is dangerous to provoke a king's wrath. Note also that the throne of a king is built on righteousness. Therefore, divine decisions should come from his mouth, and he must not sin in judgement. (Proverbs 16:10, NRSV)

4. Be diligent in labor and do not be lazy sleeping away your time, lest you fall into poverty.

5. Observe the natural inclinations of your children and try to correct their ways early where necessary.

6. Be wise and honest in business dealings, lest you are snared and trapped by dishonest people.

7. Do not be captivated by flattery of the talebearer.

8. Be patient and diligent in building wealth. Knowledge and wisdom are more valuable than precious stones, silver, and gold.

9. Do not render evil for evil but leave everything to the Lord, for vengeance belongs to God and He will repay.

10. Let your steps be ordered by the Lord and you will not stumble.

11. Strong correction may be necessary to cleanse away evil from the heart and to form the inner depths of the soul.

PRAYER: *Jehovah God of all creation, You made all things by Your wisdom out of love for humanity. Yet we are imperfect and cannot live without Your guidance, protection, counsel, and direction. So, we pray in faith and with thanksgiving in the name of Christ Jesus that You grant us every day what we need to live in peace, to live with discretion and discernment, and to honor our parents, those in authority over us, and to love one another as Christ has taught us to do. Hallelujah…Amen!*

Proverbs Chapter 21

Day #21

Dependence on God. Practice God's attributes. Follow godly principles of righteousness. Choose the simple life over wasteful lavishness and greed. Show kindness to the poor, practice humility, and promote justice. Love of pleasure and wine often lead to poverty.

1. The righteous and the faithful will eventually overcome the wicked.

2. There are some treasures that are desirable and good for the wise, but the foolish will squander and waste them.

3. Follow righteousness and mercy and you will find life and honor, for righteousness and justice are more acceptable to God than sacrifice.

4. Guard the mouth and tongue. Be humble, diligent, truthful, and listen to wise counsel so God's grace and favor will attend your way.

5. Seek the Lord in making all your plans. Search for God's guidance and direction and you will avoid foolishness that leads to failure and destruction.

6. Jehovah God has the power to control the heart of rulers, kings, and princes. So, let believers pray that the Lord will consistently and constantly do so.

7. It is good and wise to be kind to the poor, for God will see and generously reward those who give to them. But those who shut their eyes, ears, and heart to the cries of the poor will also cry themselves.

8. With wisdom, the wise overtakes a city—not by human strength.

9. The proud and haughty act with arrogance and are called "scoffers."

10. There is no wisdom, counsel, or strength that can be compared to the Lord's.

PRAYER: *Jehovah, our God, all wisdom resides in You and comes from You. We thank You that, when we ask, You are generous to give what we need. Instill in us Your wisdom, we pray, and change our hearts, O Lord God of Hosts. Lead us into paths of righteousness and truth, we beseech You. In the name of Christ Jesus of Nazareth, we lift our prayers to You in faith and with thanksgiving. Hallelujah...Amen!*

Proverbs Chapter 22

Day #22

Keep in mind the godly reputation you want to develop and be known for, because it is better than great riches in the end and place you in the presence of kings and people of influence.

1. To sow prudence, humility, generosity, kindness, truth, honesty, upright living, and caring for the poor, will lead to favor with God and with man. The generous person shall be blessed.

2. Trust in the Lord and listen to wise counsel that you will know how to answer with words of truth.

3. Jehovah God will plunder those who plunder the poor. Do not oppress them.

4. Do not foolishly make vows, shake hands, or make pledges for someone else's debt.

5. The excellent worker will be honored in the presence of kings.

6. Be reminded that both rich and poor are created by God and try to be mindful of this truth. It will help us to practice compassion and humility.

7. Those who sow iniquity will have sorrow with thorns and thistles in their way.

8. Be careful to lovingly train children up with godly principles and discipline.

9. Purity of heart and grace on the lips will win favor with kings.

10. Those who abhor the Lord will fall into the hands of immoral women. Therefore, keep your trust in the Lord and avoid such pitfalls.

PRAYER: *Creator God of heaven and earth, in Your steadfast love and mercy, help us—Your children—to build wise, godly, compassionate, humble, and discerning characters of integrity. Show us how to choose true friends who are faithful and reliable. Give us a kind and discerning heart with a willing spirit, we pray. In the name of Christ Jesus of Nazareth, we lift our prayer by faith and with thanksgiving. Hallelujah…Amen!*

Proverbs Chapter 23

Day #23

Greed, riches, the wisdom of a controlled tongue. Abuse of the poor and their property. Counsel and correction of the young that will save them from hell. Trust in God and do not envy sinners. The result of drunkenness, gluttony, and laziness. Seek wisdom, truth, instruction, and understanding. Try to make your parents proud and happy. Avoid seductive people and liars by putting your trust in God and by observing God's ways.

1. Do not greedily and foolishly overwork yourself for worldly riches, nor be envious of the rich—but be zealous for God.

2. Do not associate with winebibbers and drunks, for this will bring you to poverty, sorrow, woe, contentions, redness of eyes, deception, cause you to say and to do strange things, and keep you going back for more.

3. Righteous children make their parents happy. They give their hearts to God and observe God's ways.

4. Identify and avoid the seductresses and the liars. They can bring you to ruin.

5. Do not be gluttonous for the food of the rich nor of the stingy. Both can be harmful and insincere. Instead, wisely control your natural appetites.

6. Understand that worldly riches are unstable. But those who put their trust in the God who gives wisdom to gain wealth will be kept stable and secure.

7. Loving and wise parents will not withhold correction from their children. When they correct them, they are delivering their souls from hell.

8. Children whose hearts are wise will cause their parents to rejoice. They will not bring shame and calamity.

9. If necessary, pay to get wisdom and truth, for these are valuable in building a godly character. Observe the ways of God that you may avoid deception, sorrow, grief, shame, and disgrace.

10. Again...be reminded that wine is a mocker, strong drink is raging, and whoever is deceived thereby is not wise (Proverbs: 20:1)

PRAYER: *O Lord, Jehovah God, in Your steadfast love and mercy that endure forever, we open our hearts and minds to Your Word. By the help of Your Holy Spirit, inspire our hearts and minds to be inclined to Your will. Keep us from worldly gluttony, drunkenness, greed, bad friendships, deceptions, and foolishness of all kinds, we pray. Give us a desire and zeal for You and for Your ways, we beseech You. Change our motivations, our characters, and our behaviors we ask. In the name of Christ Jesus, the Author and Finisher of our faith and our righteousness. We lift our prayer to You, Abba/Father, and believe we have what we ask in His name. We pray: "Let your Kingdom come, and your will be done in our lives, on earth, as it is in heaven." Hallelujah...Amen!*

Proverbs Chapter 24

Day #24

Avoid the evil, deceptive, and the foolish, who try to do harm to the righteous, for God defends and sustains the righteous and protects them from stumbling. So keep faith in the faithful God and not in changeable people. And do not plan revenge, for vengeance belongs to God and God will repay.

1. Avoid the violent troublemaker.

2. Build your life/house with wisdom, knowledge, and understanding as precious furnishings.

3. Seek wise counsel before waging war, so you might find safety and gain victory.

4. In the day of adversity, maintain strength through faith in God, who knows and weighs the heart to render each according to their deeds.

5. Do not plot evil against the righteous, for the lamp of the wicked shall be put out.

6. Fear God and respect the king so that you do not come to ruin.

7. Do not take sides with the wicked against the righteous, for you will come to calamity with them.

8. Laziness, sleep, and slumber will bring a person to poverty and ruin.

61

9. In days of adversity, do not faint but seek strength from the Lord to sustain you.

10. Work for justice and against evil, and God will keep your soul and reward you in due season.

11. Unlike the wicked, if a righteous person falls seven times, be assured that the Lord will raise him up.

12. Do not envy evildoers, for their end will not be good.

13. Laziness and idleness lead to brokenness and poverty, So be diligent and faithful to God, in your work, and in your service.

PRAYER: *Come, Holy Spirit, and breathe into us the wisdom of our Creator, we pray. Transform our minds, build our characters, and make us diligent, energized, and discerning, we ask. Teach us how to build a life based on righteousness and not on wickedness, on truth and not on what is false. Keep us from ruination and poverty, O Jehovah, our God, for all our strength is in You and all wisdom comes from You. In the name of Christ Jesus, we ask that You might give to us what we need for we seek that we shall find what is eternal. We knock so that You may open unto us these blessings and pour them into us abundantly. Hallelujah...Amen!*

Proverbs Chapter 25

Day #25

Avoid quarrels, respect the authority of kings/rulers. —It is God's right to keep certain things secret, but it is up to the king to search them out. Observe and practice social graces true loyalty, and humility.

1. When the wicked are removed from the king's presence, it is like purifying dross from silver jewelry, and the king's throne will be established in righteousness.

2. Practice humility by taking the lower place that you might be exalted, instead of being demoted to a lower place and be embarrassed.

3. Avoid going to the worldly court to resolve a problem with a relative or friend. First try using diplomacy and debate, lest you expose yourself to shame and ruin your reputation.

4. Let your words be as apples of gold set in silver. It will make a rebuke acceptable to an obedient ear. A gentle tongue is very effective in difficult situations.

5. A faithful servant is like refreshing snow at harvest to his master. Those who serve or work as unto God will be rewarded accordingly.

6. Even honey can be too clawing, so eat only enough. In other words, do all things in moderation and do not overindulge.

7. Do not be in your neighbor's house too often. He might become tired of you and hate you.

8. A false witness and an unfaithful person are both cause for deep pains and wounds to the soul of the innocent and the guiltless.

9. Feed your enemy and give them drink, for so you find favor with God and stir the conscience of those who hate you.

10. Do not back-bite with your tongue or be contentious with your mouth. This will cause malice and misery.

11. Good news from a far country is like fresh cold water to the soul.

12. Do not boast and seek your own glory; but keep rule over your own spirit and have self-control. Otherwise, you will be like a city with broken down walls which is open to destruction.

PRAYER: *Jehovah God in Trinity, in Your steadfast love and mercy, make us wise, diligent, faithful, true, self-controlled, humble, and steadfast, we pray. Keep our tongues from gossip, contentions, and strife, we beseech You. Put right words in our mouths, we ask, and help us not to seek revenge but to do good to those who make themselves our enemies. Let our tongues speak wisely and gently into situations, especially when a rebuke is necessary. O Lord, keep a guard over our lips and a watch over our tongues, we beseech You. In the name of Christ Jesus, we lift these prayers in faith and with thanksgiving, and look forward to a changed personality, new attitude, a wise tongue, and all that makes us wise and blesse, children of God. Hallelujah…Amen!*

Proverbs Chapter 26

Day #26

Identify and avoid the foolish, the tattlers, the sluggards, and the meddlesome ones.

1. Those who meddle in the affairs and quarrels of others do so to their own detriment and are undeserving of honor.

2. There is peace where there is no tattler or talebearer.

3. Observe the lazy, who create excuses for not producing. They refuse to get out of bed and are wise in their own eyes.

4. Whoever digs a pit or rolls a stone to obstruct or ensnare others will fall into it himself.

5. God will not allow an undeserved curse to take effect. Therefore, those who are wrongfully cursed receive mercy, compassion, and favor with God.

6. Do not engage with foolish people in arguments, for you will become just like them, and they will appear to be wise in their own eyes.

7. A talebearer is dangerous among others, but he/she will be exposed publicly. Also, know that a flattering tongue works ruin. So, try not to be known as such.

8. Where there is no wood or someone to stoke a fire, strife ceases. So, do not start an argument with a neighbor and claim it was a joke.

9. Those who try to cover hatred by deceit will be found out publicly.

PRAYER: *Holy God of heaven and earth, in Your loving-kindness and tender mercies, keep us from being meddlers, talebearers, lazy, or quarrelsome, we pray. Make us all that we ought to be and help us to do what we ought to do that pleases You. Help us, we beseech You, to do what causes us to be blessed so that we may become a blessing. Let Your kingdom come in our lives, and Your will be done on earth as it is in heaven, we pray. We receive these favors by faith and with thanksgiving in the name of Christ Jesus. Hallelujah…Amen!*

Proverbs Chapter 27

Day #27

Understand the folly of boasting, self-praise, wrath, anger, and jealousy. Live well with neighbors and avoid quarrels.

1. Entrust your plans into the hands of God and do not boast or worry about tomorrow, for you do not know what is in store.

2. Do not engage in self-praise. It is a sign of arrogance and pride. Let others praise you.

3. Be alert to deceptive praise, jealousy, and the kisses of an enemy. It is better to have and to heed the open rebuke of a true friend than to accept flattery as true praise from a deceiver.

4. Sincere and sweet friendships delight the heart with wise counsel.

5. If trouble and calamity strike, be careful not to wear out a friend, brother, or neighbor by frequently going to their house with complaints and distress. Instead, be quiet, meditate on the Word of God, and offer worship and praise to the Lord.

6. When you see trouble and danger ahead, do all you can to avoid it, and do not foolishly or unwittingly run into it to your own detriment.

7. A contentious person is like the annoyance of dripping rain that cannot be restrained. It causes discomfort and misery in homes, families, and other relationships.

8. True friends sharpen one another, and a faithful servant is honored by his/her master.

9. It is almost impossible to remove foolishness from a fool even if you grind him/her like mortar in a pestle.

10. Be diligent in attending to your flock [affairs/ business] to protect your well-being and possessions, for riches do not last forever. When everything is carefully protected and cared for, then the fields will produce herbs and the lambs will provide clothing, milk, food, and nourishment for one's household. Therefore, be diligent, attentive, and faithful in all that you do, so that there will be plenty of provision at all times.

11. Good friendships are like honey that delight the heart. They are to be nurtured and not forsaken. As iron sharpens iron, so true friends lift the countenance of one another.

PRAYER: *Jehovah God of all wisdom, knowledge, and understanding, we ask, seek, and knock for the help of the Holy Spirit to develop, to maintain, and to retain the ability to discern sincere friends, and to be diligent in acquiring and protecting the character, skills, and abilities that will produce prosperity and well-being. Teach us how to avoid contentions, evil, and all manner of dangerous situations, so we can have peace. In the name of Christ Jesus Your Son, we lift our prayer in faith, trusting that You are releasing to us more than we could ever imagine, ask, or think. Hallelujah...Amen!*

Proverbs Chapter 28

Day #28

Lawlessness, the oppression of the poor, injustice, dishonesty usury, extortion, and a lack of wisdom are offensive to God and hurtful to others. But love and compassion cover errors and do not bring others to open shame. So do not put incompetent rulers in authority because they will cause great oppression.

1. Rulers and people of dishonest and oppressive character are insensitive to the poor. They lack understanding and godly wisdom. Therefore, they will reap the disfavor of a Holy God, but the righteous will rejoice with great glory.

2. Whoever confesses his/her sins and forsakes them will prosper and be granted mercy.

3. The diligent, faithful, and blameless person will abound in blessings.

4. Those who hasten to be rich will stumble.

5. One who steals from parents, saying it is no transgression, is foolish and destructive.

6. Whoever walks wisely, according to the Word of God, and gives to the poor will be delivered from curses and will prosper.

7. Cultivate good relationships with neighbors, be a good friend, and value your own friends.

8. Wealth gained by extortion and usury is offensive to God, and it will not last; but the blameless will inherit what is good.

9. The wicked is always suspicious of others and flees when no one is in pursuit, but the righteous are confident and bold. When the righteous rise, the people flourish.

10. Those who labor diligently and honestly will have plenty.

11. A strong rebuke is better in the end than a flattering tongue.

12. Those who give to the poor will not be in want, for Jehovah God will sustain them.

PRAYER: *Jehovah God of all generosity and kindness, in Your mercy, incline our hearts and minds to confess our sins and not to hide them, lest our prayers go unanswered. Help us and all who prosper to be mindful of the poor and needy, we beseech You in the name of Christ Jesus. Change the hearts and minds of those who oppress the weak, the orphans, and the widows, we pray. In Your compassion, lift the weight of injustice from the backs of all who are oppressed and deliver them from evil. Let the righteous be placed in positions of authority and not the wicked. We lift our prayers to You with thanksgiving in the name of Christ Jesus Your Son and our Savior. Hallelujah...Amen!*

Proverbs Chapter 29

Day #29

Show respect for Civil government, practice wise counsel in the home, and correct children. Lead by example. Disobedience to wise counsel and rebuke will result in serious consequences in one's life.

1. When the righteous rule with justice, wisdom, and integrity, the people rejoice and prosper.

2. A wise ruler pays no attention to the lies of scoffers and foolish people but judges the poor with truth, and his throne is established forever.

3. Children left to themselves without parental counsel and guidance will bring shame. If children are corrected, they will become a delight to the souls of their parents.

4. Where there is spiritual darkness and lack of wisdom, people rebel against the law and there is no restraint in the society.

5. Do not conspire with thieves and robbers, for you will share in their guilt and punishment.

6. Rulers who accept bribes tarnish their reputation and weaken their authority.

7. The wise should not contend with the foolish, for it is futile and useless to do so.

8. Hastiness, anger, pride, and impatience stir up strife, but the humble seek peace and retain honor.

9. Though people seek favor from earthly rulers, it is the Lord who grants true justice.

PRAYER: *Omniscient God, look upon the nations, upon Your world, upon us, and upon our homes, we pray. Grant wisdom to all who are in authority, we beseech You. Pour out Your Spirit upon us and cause us all to seek Your face and find wisdom to lead with righteous justice, humility, courage, and with peace. Help us and our leaders to lead with compassion, insight, prudence, and discernment, we ask. In the name of Christ Jesus, the Author and Finisher of our faith, we lift our prayers in faith and with thanksgiving to You, Abba/Father. Hallelujah... Amen!*

Proverbs Chapter 30

Day #30

The confession of Agur in this chapter acknowledges his own foolishness and lack of knowledge of the Holy One. —Yet, he asks some very deep theological questions concerning ascension, creation, and what is the name of God's son. —He wrote these questions hundreds of years before Christ came to earth in flesh. This is the way all of us should be humble students in our search for God and for wisdom.

1. Agur recognizes his own insignificance and ignorance when compared to the omniscient, omnipotent, omnipresent Creator of the universe. With Him, there is no comparison at all.

2. Agur declares that the purity of the Word of God is a shield to all who take refuge in God. Therefore, do not add or subtract from God's Law, Word, or Commandments.

3. He asks the Lord to keep him from false words and to grant him enough provision daily so that he would not steal.

4. He does not want to amass too much wealth that he forgets God. This is when temptation is most likely to overtake and ruin people. (Unless they are rooted in the Word and wisdom of God.)

5. He is critical of a depraved, cruel, and lawless generation, who curses parents, who are prideful and arrogant in their own eyes (a very harsh critique!). Their teeth are like swords. They have fangs like knives, and they devour the poor among them.

6. They are like leeches who are never satisfied—saying: "Give, give!"

7. Like the grave, the barren womb, scorched earth, and fire, there is never enough for them.

8. He speaks repeatedly of three and four things poetically which amaze and fascinate him: the way of the eagle in the sky, the way of the serpent on a rock, the way of a ship in the sea...

9. Agur is perturbed by the behavior of an adulterous woman who becomes married and thinks she has done nothing wrong, a servant who becomes a ruler, a maid who succeeds her mistress, and a fool when filled with food.

10. He admires the innate wisdom of the tiny ants that, in the summer, prepare food for the winter, the rock badgers that make their dwelling in the crags, the locusts that advance in ordered ranks, the spiders that live in kings' palaces, the fearless and mighty strides of a lion, the greyhound, the male goat, and the king whose troops obey him. We are invited to observe and to do likewise.

11. If anyone has become puffed up with pride and has devised evil against another, do not let it fester and create strife, but turn from it and repent.

12. The ways of the incomprehensible God can be learned from simple and small animals and insects in creation. Much can be learned from them if we take time to observe.

PRAYER: *O Jehovah, our God, like Agur, we confess our lack of wisdom, knowledge, and understanding, and we repent. We come humbly, seeking Your face and asking that You will release what we need to make us wiser, more humble, more truthful, considerate, kind, loving, faithful, merciful, compassionate, and diligent. Help us to learn from the seemingly small and insignificant animals by observing their natural instincts that cause them to be disciplined, organized, to survive, and even to thrive. You are the only great and Holy One. Help us, we pray, to recognize our smallness in Your sight, and to learn from Your Word all that will make us fulfill our purpose here on earth. In the name of Christ Jesus, we lift these prayers in faith and with thanksgiving. Hallelujah... Amen!*

Proverbs Chapter 31

Day #31

The Proverb of King Lemuel's mother is one all mothers may adopt for their children as they grow up in society and begin to make meaningful and serious life decisions about careers, leadership, and family life.

1. Do not give your strength to women, your ways to drinking of strong drink, and do not pervert justice and oppress the poor.

2. Intervene on behalf of the voiceless, and on behalf of those appointed to die. Open your mouth and judge righteously, pleading the cause of the poor.

3. She teaches him about the value and qualities of a virtuous wife. She is diligent, industrious, faithful, an entrepreneur, an excellent home manager, care giver, mother, and wife; creative, strong, well dressed in fine linen, and makes herself, her home, and her family beautiful. She opens her mouth with wisdom and with the law of kindness. She is never idle. Her children arise and call her blessed.

4. Most of all, she is a woman who fears the Lord. Her works praise her in the community, and she enjoys the fruit of her labor.

5. Her husband honors her, and she makes him proud and well respected in the community.

6. She extends her hands to the poor and needy.

7. Perhaps it may be helpful to give strong drink to those who are perishing in misery that they may be comforted, but it is not good for rulers and kings.

PRAYER: *Ever-loving and eternal God, Jesus is the Word made flesh. He is the Author and Finisher of our faith. Without His help and the work of the Holy Spirit, we are confused and lost. We need Your wisdom, guidance, and direction in every area of our lives, in our governments, our churches, our homes, our schools, in marriages, in our families and relationships. We love You, who first loved us and gave Your Son to die for our sins so that we will have salvation and all the good things that are made available to us. Help us now, we pray, to grow in grace through our faith in Him. Let the wisdom, knowledge, and understanding that are ours be made manifest now in our lives at every level. For these blessings, we give thanks by faith, because we ask all things in the blessed and precious name of Christ Jesus. Hallelujah…Amen!*

Taken after the Easter Sunday worship at St. John the Divine in NYC (2023) --where I often worship since my retirement.

A Brief Summary And Reflection

Throughout the Book of Proverbs, we are shown the difference between the character of the wise versus that of the foolish.

THE FOOLISH: They say there is no God. They hate counsel, are ignorant of the Word of God, are arrogant, oppress the poor and weak, talk more than they listen, and partial to the rich; are tattlers and tale bearers, contentious, and sexually immoral; they lack integrity and self-control, are disrespectful to parents, make poor business choices by making pledges and vows for the debt of others, hasty; they are offensive in their language, join with violent friends, full of flattery, and are dishonest, untrustworthy, double-minded, unstable, greedy, jealous, envious, unkind; cause strife wherever they go; are murderers, adulterers, and much more.

BUT THE WISE are the opposite. They believe and know that: God is, God was, and God exists forever. God is holy, omnipotent, omnipresent, omniscient, and God exists in Trinity—Father, Son, and Holy Spirit. They fear and reverence Jehovah as the true and living God, Creator, Sustainer, and Provider. They know that Jehovah God is Almighty. They help the poor, discipline their children, make wise business choices, are selective in making friends, know to seek God in making plans for their lives, families, and business; are diligent in their work, compassionate, avoid quarrels, seek wise counsel, respect civil authorities, know how to identify and avoid seduction, care for the well-being of their family, know that they should return the tithe to God and do so faithfully, are obedient and teachable, seek justice, care for widows and orphans, are gracious, and reliable.

On our earthly journey, may we strive to be in the category of the wise and righteous that we might receive a heavenly and eternal reward.

Postscript

In January of 2020, just after Reverend Brenda R. Berry retired at the end of 2019, she felt led to do a study of the Book of Proverbs. At that time, she had no plans to make it into a book of her own. Rev. Berry thought she would do it for her own edification. But with all the chaos and terror of the COVID-19 Pandemic, the political turmoil, the social unrest, blatant injustice, irrational hate, violence, arrogance, selfishness, foolishness, sickness, and disease, it occurred to her that something spiritual, moral, and foundational was out of order or had been removed.

After reading through Proverbs on her own and making notes, Rev. Berry invited a small group of people to join her in a weekly conference call Bible study with reflections, discussions, and prayer. It was not until early 2021 that the idea of a book began to emerge. She saw the lack of biblical understanding, knowledge, and godly wisdom that seemed to be at the root of much of the upheaval, trauma, fear, and evil still happening in the world and environment today. However, it did not just start a year or two ago. The erosion has been happening for more than a decade. So, she asks the question: "Wisdom...Where Are You?" Wisdom has been calling out to humanity globally, nationally, locally, and otherwise; but she has been ignored. So, it seems people have been left to go their own ways, and what there is now may be in some way due to the lack of biblical wisdom, knowledge, understanding, and training.

The Prophet Isaiah, speaking for God, is calling out to everyone who thirsts, saying: "Come to the waters...Come buy milk and honey without money and without price...Listen to Me and eat what is good...Incline your ear and come to Me. Hear and your soul shall live" (Isaiah 55:1-3). Again, Proverbs 4:7 tells all who read that, "Wisdom is the principal thing."

Suggested Activity

- Decide how you will begin to faithfully inscribe these biblical truths to yourself personally, and how you will try to instill them in the hearts and minds of your children, family, relatives, and friends.

- Explain how this study has impacted your thinking.

If you had these lessons instilled in your heart and mind earlier, would you have managed life's choices differently? How so?

CRITIQUE:

In what way has this study been helpful? Would you recommend it to anyone else?

How could this study be improved and shared?

Prepared by:
Rev. Brenda R. Berry: B.A., M.Div.
Pastor Emeritus—Univ. Hts. Presby. Chr.
Bronx, NY.
(Not to be duplicated without permission)

About The Author

Having been a pastor for over eighteen years, an elementary school teacher and a high school English teacher for a brief time in my earlier years, as well as an employee working in a major telecommunications company from a Key-Punch Clerk level to Staff and Project Manager at the Company's Headquarters for twenty- three years, I believe I have observed a need for godly wisdom to be specifically taught to the young as well as to many adults. (Not just by Osmosis-but intentionally taught by wise counselors or teachers as well as by parents.) Like Agur I can say that in my early years I learned a lot of Scripture verses, attended church regularly, and did some Bible Studies along the way. That seemed to have sustained me for a while; but when the storms of life hit, application became necessary. Discernment, insight, prudence, and understanding became critical for my survival and there wasn't enough of it, nor were there wise counselors who could help. It seemed that despite all my hard work and best efforts, everything was caving in around me. I could not discern what was wrong. My sons and I were in turmoil. We were going to church but that was not enough. I began to search and to seek the LORD more intentionally, and the Holy Spirit began to draw me to deeper understanding, knowledge, and to the wisdom of God.

One night out of utter frustration I called out to God and asked "Lord, what is this all about? Why are these things happening to me? What did I do to deserve all this?" I lay back on my bed not expecting anything to happen. But as my spirit began to rest, I heard a whisper saying: "Isaiah 54." I jumped up and got the Bible. I read the entire chapter and was somewhat mesmerized by it all. The promises of beautiful, precious stones and adornment, the promises of mercy, compassion, love, and kindness…etc., surprised me and encouraged me. I was shocked to know that Jehovah God really hears and really speaks!!! However, I was particularly drawn to verse 6 which says: "For the LORD has called you as a woman forsaken and grieved in spirit, like a youthful wife when you were refused, says Your God…" I took this literally because it directly pointed to and addressed what I was going through at that time.

I can't say that I have arrived, but at the very least I can say that my eyes, my ears, and my heart have become more open and receptive, more disciplined in studying, learning, interpreting, applying, in preaching, teaching, and in sharing the Word of God. It's value and worth in my daily life have developed and matured over time. This is a life-long endeavor, and there is always more to know and to apply for life and for living. I hope and trust that these lessons and prayers with faith will help those who are seeking understanding and are searching for true wisdom.

Upper Room in Jerusalem, where Pentecost happened, visited in the year 2000 and shared in Holy Communion.

.

Milton Keynes UK
Ingram Content Group UK Ltd.
UKHW050756020124
435290UK00010B/80